Christmas Underwear

To the Jackson family—
May you always cherish your family traditions!
much love—
♡ Keri Measom-Francis
2019

BY KERI MEASOM-FRANCIS
ILLUSTRATED BY ADDISON WELCH

Dedication Page

Dedicated to my mom and dad: my first and best teachers. KMF
To little Wendy Elmer. AW

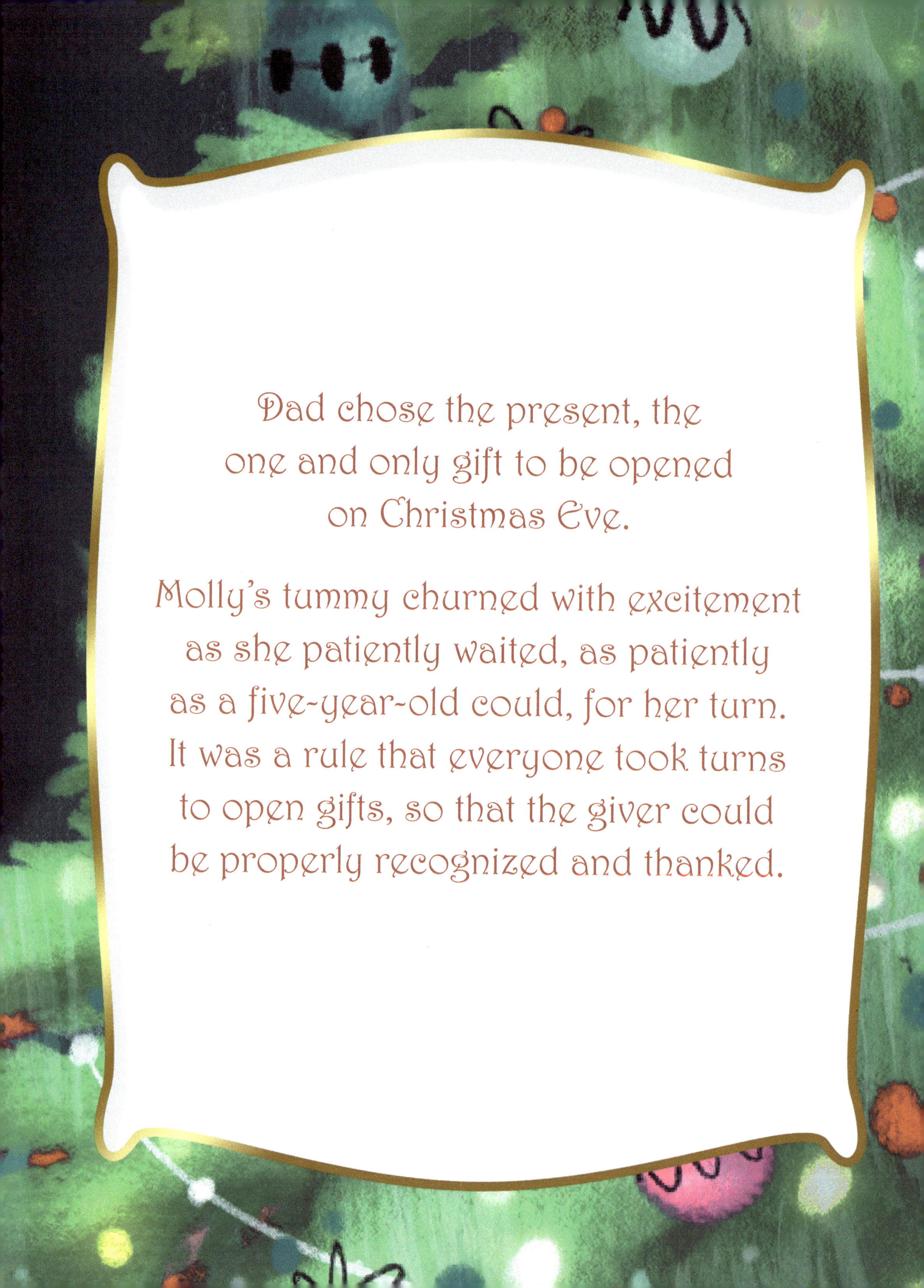

Dad chose the present, the
one and only gift to be opened
on Christmas Eve.

Molly's tummy churned with excitement as she patiently waited, as patiently as a five-year-old could, for her turn. It was a rule that everyone took turns to open gifts, so that the giver could be properly recognized and thanked.

Wrapped in red and green paper sat her one special gift. A sparkly red bow, Molly's favorite color, adorned the top of the package.

"Go ahead and open it Molly," coaxed her dad with a slight grin. "It's your turn."

Peeling back the paper ever so carefully (in case Grandma Joy wanted to save it) Molly began unwrapping. She felt something soft and squishy and imagined a new stuffed animal or some fuzzy slippers.

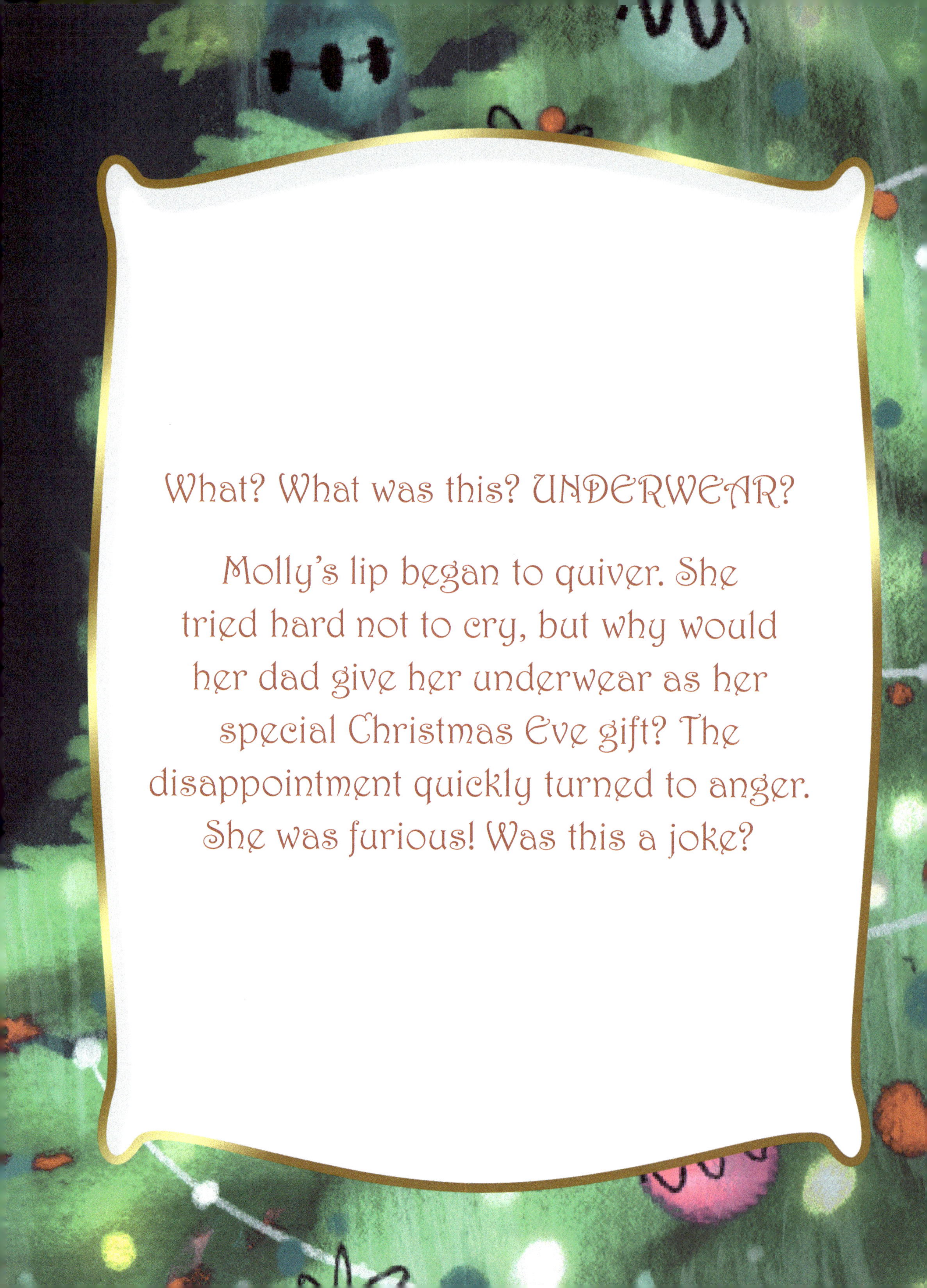

What? What was this? UNDERWEAR?

Molly's lip began to quiver. She tried hard not to cry, but why would her dad give her underwear as her special Christmas Eve gift? The disappointment quickly turned to anger. She was furious! Was this a joke?

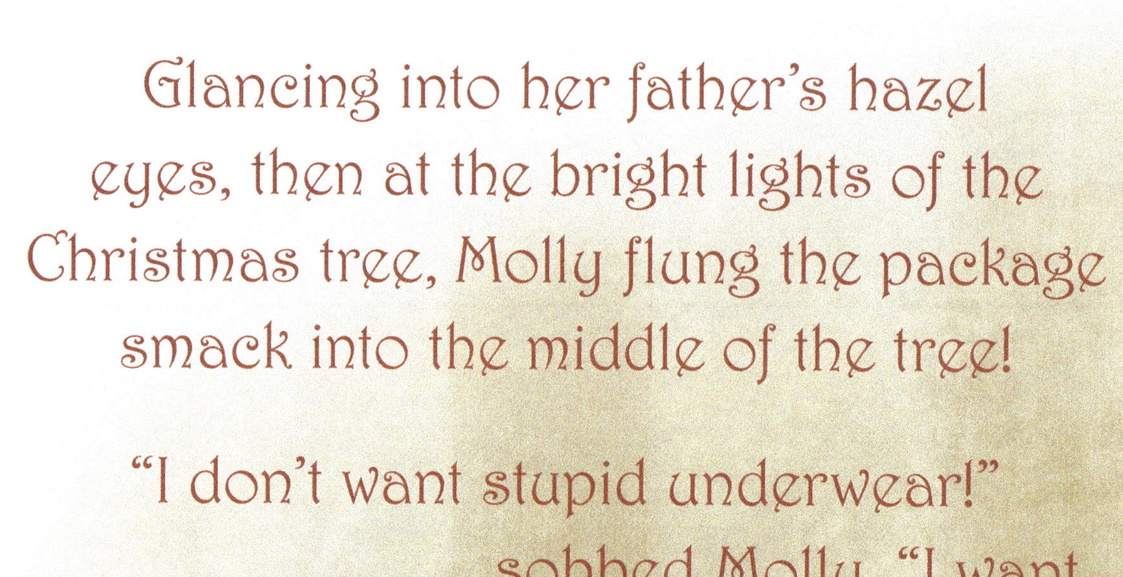

Glancing into her father's hazel eyes, then at the bright lights of the Christmas tree, Molly flung the package smack into the middle of the tree!

"I don't want stupid underwear!" sobbed Molly. "I want a different present!"

Silence.

The family froze. None of the other children had complained. In fact, they had graciously thanked their parents. Suddenly, Molly was sick inside. Every member of her family was glaring at her. Dad slowly motioned her to come and sit on his knee.

In a firm but friendly voice dad spoke, "When I was a little boy we were very poor. One particular holiday season will forever be etched in my memory. Grandpa George had died and Grandma was doing everything she could just to keep our growing bodies fed. Our kind neighbors and friends donated food and small amounts of money to assist us, but there was no money for extra gifts. On Christmas morning, my sisters and I were surprised to be gifted one beautifully wrapped present. Can you guess what our present was?"

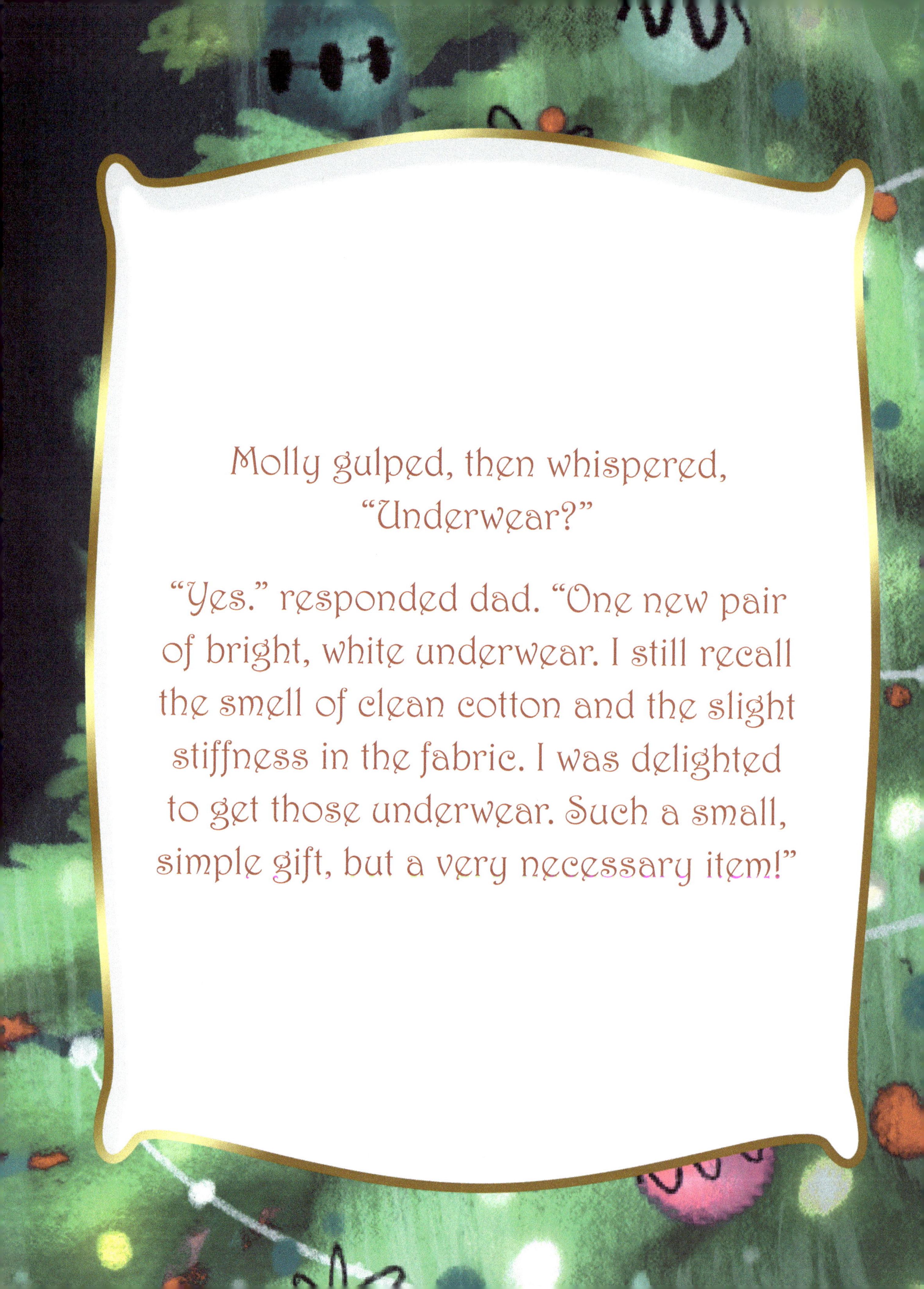

Molly gulped, then whispered, "Underwear?"

"Yes." responded dad. "One new pair of bright, white underwear. I still recall the smell of clean cotton and the slight stiffness in the fabric. I was delighted to get those underwear. Such a small, simple gift, but a very necessary item!"

Dad chuckled and gazed lovingly at Molly. “A gift is special no matter what, because someone thought enough about you to give it to you. Someone spent time and energy to choose the perfect present just for you, and whether you like it or not, it is still a gift. I want you to be grateful for every gift, be it a new doll or a shiny bike, a t-shirt or new underwear, whether you like it or not. Gratitude is the key to abundance and my Christmas wish is that you will always be grateful and remember, any gift is special because it is a gift.”

Covering her face with two tiny hands, Molly snuggled in closer to her dad. Still crying with embarrassment and regret she mustered up enough courage to glance at the family, "I am sorry. I am really sorry."

As only a loving father can, Molly's dad squoze her tightly. "I know you are. I love you little bug."

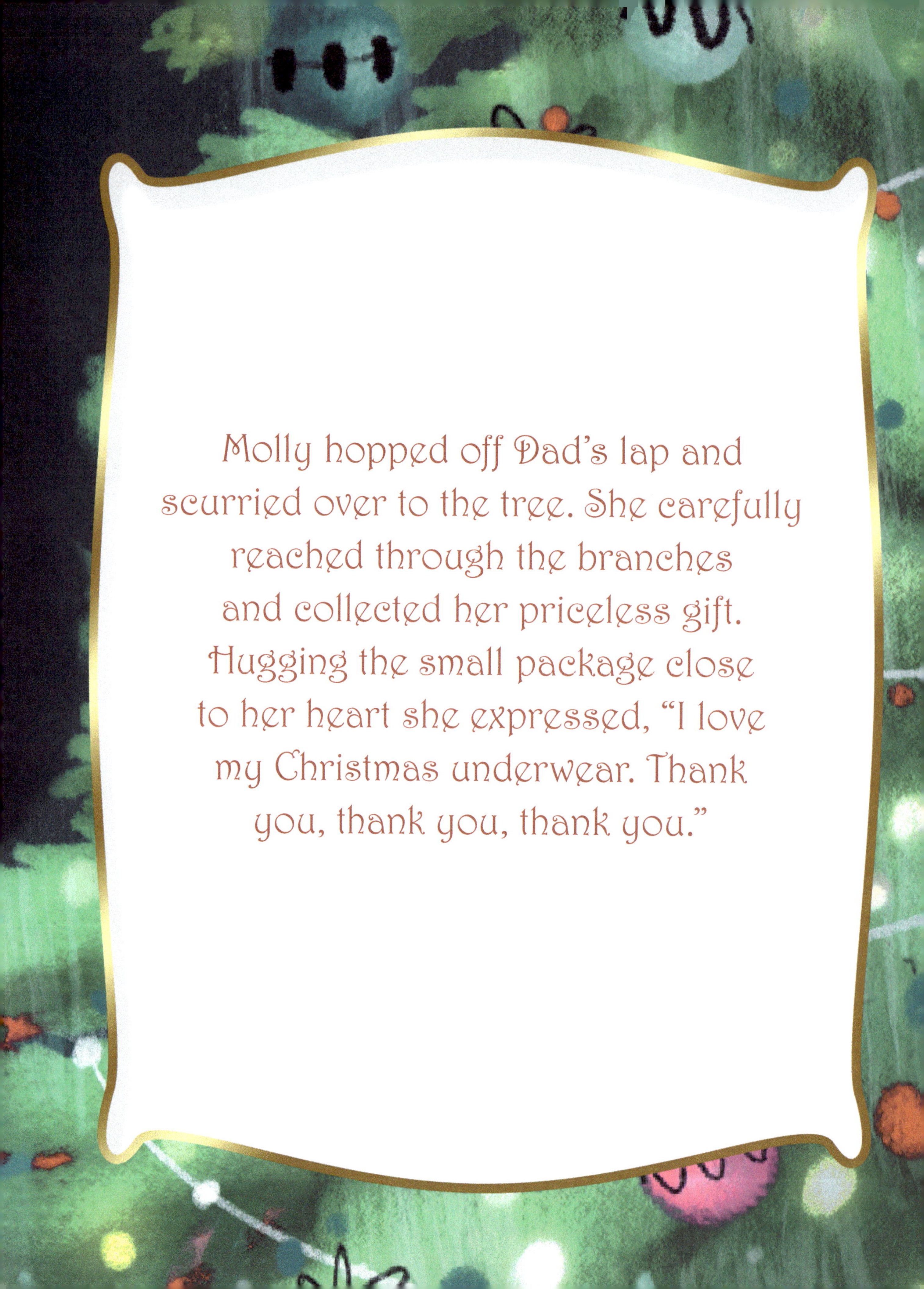

Molly hopped off Dad's lap and scurried over to the tree. She carefully reached through the branches and collected her priceless gift. Hugging the small package close to her heart she expressed, "I love my Christmas underwear. Thank you, thank you, thank you."

Afterword:

Every Christmas thereafter Molly anxiously awaited her Christmas Eve gift, and yes, it was always underwear. She graciously thanked the giver and remembered her father's wise words, "Any gift is special because it is a gift."

About the Author:

Keri Measom-Francis has been a public educator for over 24 years. She passionately engages her students and has inspired thousands to tell their unique stories through writing. Currently she teaches and learns with future educators at Utah Valley University. A longtime resident of Utah, Keri enjoys spending time with her husband, Scott, and children McKenna (Tyler), Saige, and Tess. Christmas Underwear is based on one of Keri's childhood experiences when she indeed chucked her gift into the Christmas tree. The story has been retold every Christmas Eve and her children receive a special gift every December 24th. Can you guess what it is?

About the Illustrator:

Addison Welch is a digital artist and entrepreneur living the dream in Salt Lake City, Utah. He loves hanging out with his wife Bre, his coolest son Alfie, and his sweet baby Poppy! Check out more of his work on Instagram @addisonwelchart. Addison is also the illustrator of another children's book entitled, Once I Went A Swimmin'.

"Any gift is special
because it is a gift."

CPSIA information can be obtained
at www.ICGtesting.com
Printed in the USA
BVHW022002130919
558092BV00002B/2/P

9 781728 323428

AuthorHouse™
1663 Liberty Drive
Bloomington, IN 47403
www.authorhouse.com
Phone: 1 (800) 839-8640

Published by AuthorHouse 08/14/2019

ISBN: 978-1-7283-2340-4 (sc)
ISBN: 978-1-7283-2342-8 (hc)
ISBN: 978-1-7283-2341-1 (e)

Print information available on the last page.

authorHOUSE®